Johann Strauss
(1825–1899)

Waltzes

Valses

Walzer

for piano • pour piano • für Klavier

K 141

INDEX

Morgenblätter, Op. 279 4
Morning Papers – Journaux du matin

An der schönen blauen Donau, Op. 314 14
By the Beautiful Blue Danube – Le beau Danube bleu

Künstlerleben, Op. 316 24
Artist's Life – La Vie d'Artiste

Geschichten aus dem Wienerwald, Op. 325 34
Tales from the Vienna Woods – Légendes de la forêt viennoise

Wein, Weib und Gesang, Op. 333 47
Wine, Women and Song – Aimer, boire et chanter

Wiener Blut, Op. 354 56
Vienna Blood – Sang viennois

Du und Du, Op. 367 66
Walzer nach Motiven der Operette "Die Fledermaus"
Thou and Thou, too
Waltz on themes from the operetta "The Bat"
Toi et toi
Valse d'après des motifs de «La chauve-souris»

Cagliostro-Walzer, Op. 370 75
Cagliostro Waltz – Valse de Cagliostro

Rosen aus dem Süden, Op. 388 86
Roses from the South – Roses du sud

Kuß-Walzer, Op. 400 97
Kiss Waltz – Valse du baiser

Frühlingsstimmen, Op. 410 106
Voices of Spring – Voix du printemps

Schatz-Walzer, Op. 418 113
Treasure Waltz – Valse du trésor

Kaiser-Walzer, Op. 437 122
Emperor Waltz – Valse de l'Empereur

Morgenblätter
Op. 279

Introduction
Allegro

Tempo di Valse

Walzer I

Walzer I D. C. al Fine e poi Walzer II

An der schönen blauen Donau

Op. 314

Coda

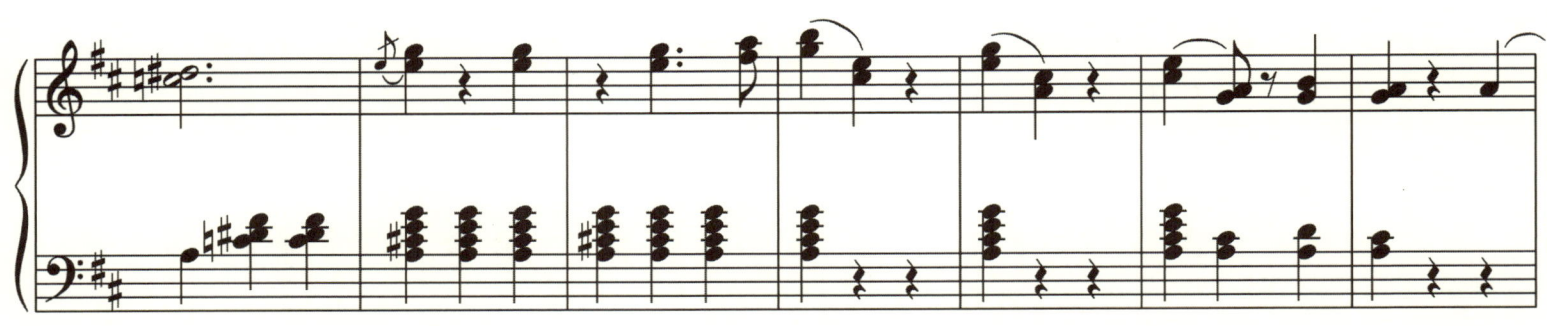

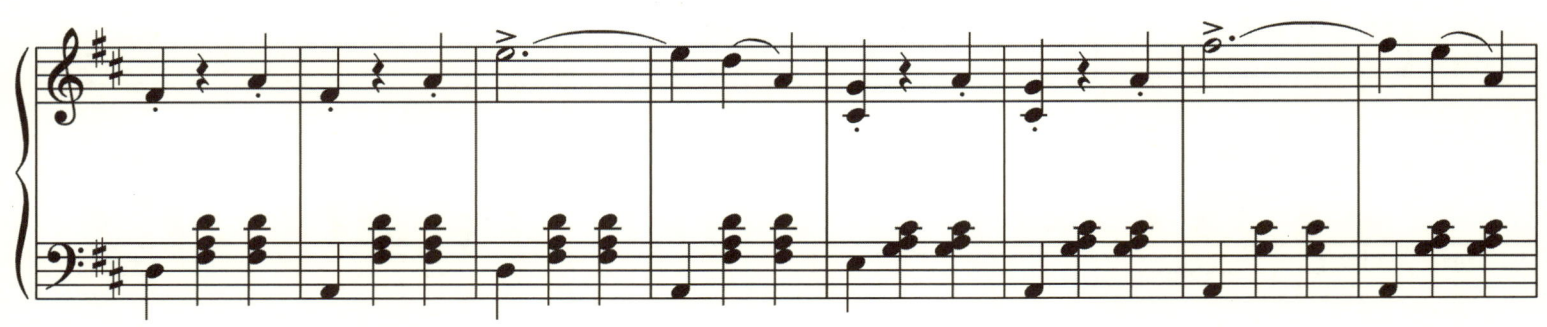

Künstlerleben
Op. 316

Walzer I

Walzer II

Walzer IV

Geschichten aus dem Wienerwald
Op. 325

Introduction
Tempo di Valse

Wein, Weib und Gesang

Op. 333.

Introduction
Andante, quasi religioso

Walzer II

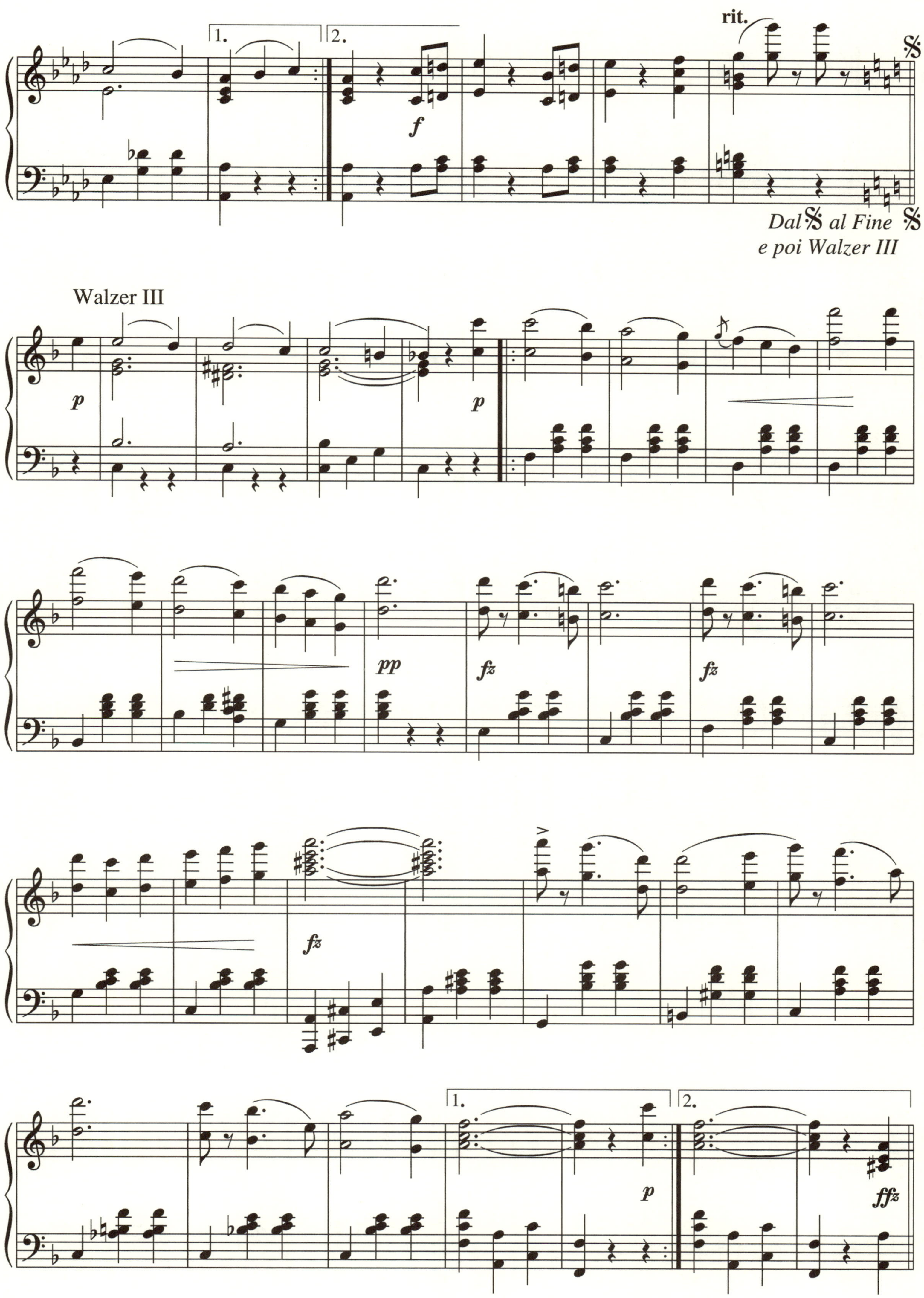

Dal 𝄋 al Fine 𝄋
e poi Walzer III

Walzer III

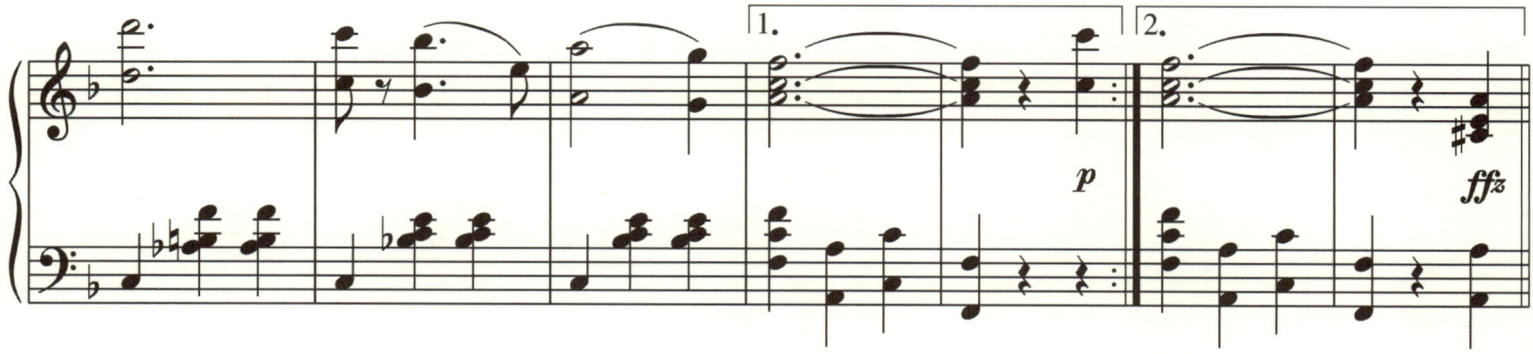

Wiener Blut
Op. 354.

Introduction
Allegro moderato

Du und Du
Walzer nach Motiven der Operette "Die Fledermaus"
Op. 367

Cagliostro - Walzer
Op.370

Introduction
Tempo di Marcia

Walzer III

Rosen aus dem Süden
Op. 388

Introduction
Andantino

Kuß - Walzer
Op. 400

Frühlingsstimmen
Op.410

Schatz - Walzer
Op. 418

Walzer I

Kaiser - Walzer
Op.437

Introduction
Langsames Marschtempo

MUSICA PIANO

OVER 25.000 PAGES OF PIANO MUSIC SHEETS ONLINE

Bach, Beethoven, Brahms, Chopin, Czerny, Debussy, Gershwin, Dvořák, Grieg, Haydn, Joplin, Lyadov, Mendelssohn-Bartholdy, Mozart, Mussorgsky, Purcell, Schubert, Schumann, Scriabin, Tchaikovsky and many more

K 141

try the web version
www.musicapiano.com

KÖNEMANN

© 2018 koenemann.com GmbH
www.koenemann.com

Piano arrangement: Miklós Szalay-Kiskamoni
Responsible co-editor: István Máriássy
Technical editor: Desző Varga
Engraved by Kottamester Bt., Budapest

critical notes available on www.frechmann.com

ISBN 978-3-7419-1527-7

Printed in China by Reliance Printing

K 141